The Loving Heart

Insights based on the writings of Janette Oke

The Loving Heart

Copyright © 1992, 1995, Janette Oke

Published by Garborg's Heart 'n Home
P.O. Box 20132, Bloomington, MN 55420

The Loving Heart contains excerpts from The Father Who Calls (© 1988), The Father of Love (© 1989), and Father of My Heart (© 1990), books which share spiritual insights based on Janette Oke's writings. The particular Janette Oke book and the page number from which these insights are gained is noted. The Loving Heart is published with the permission of Bethany House Publishers, Minneapolis, MN.

All rights reserved. No part of this book may be reproduced in any form without permission in writing from the publisher.

Scripture quotations marked NIV are taken from the HOLY BIBLE, NEW INTERNATIONAL VERSION® NIV®. Copyright © 1973, 1978, 1984 by International Bible Society. All rights reserved.

SPCN 5-5044-0283-2

A quiet place is a good place to find out God's angle on any problem.

ONCE UPON A SUMMER PP. 9,10

Think on these things.

PHILIPPIANS 4:8 KJV

January 1

Now glory be to God, who by his mighty power at work within us is able to do far more than we would ever dare to ask or even dream of—infinitely beyond our highest prayers, desires, thoughts, or hopes.

EPHESIANS 3:20 TLB

December 31

When we feel someone else's pain, we can help to lessen it.

ONCE UPON A SUMMER PP. 11,12

If one falls down, his friend can help him up.

ECCLESIASTES 4:10 NIV

January 2

I am still confident of this: I will see the goodness of the Lord in the land of the living. Wait for the Lord; be strong and take heart and wait for the Lord.

Psalm 27:13,14 NIV

December 30

We will never regret doing
the things we know we should do.

ONCE UPON A SUMMER pp. 12,13

The statutes of the Lord are right, rejoicing the heart.

PSALM 19:8 KJV

January 3

*O*nly God knows whether or not our confession is sincere.

The Winds of Autumn pp. 176,177

Let us draw near to God with a sincere heart in full assurance of faith, having our hearts sprinkled to cleanse us from a guilty conscience.

Hebrews 10:22 niv

December 29

No one ever outgrows the need for a mother's love.

ONCE UPON A SUMMER PP. 13,14

*Honor your father and mother,...
that it may go well with you.*

DEUTERONOMY 5:16 NIV

January 4

𝒪ur bodies deteriorate in this life, but in the life to come they will be transformed.

WHEN BREAKS THE DAWN PP. 101, 102

The Lord Jesus Christ...will transform our lowly bodies so that they will be like his glorious body.

PHILIPPIANS 3:20,21 NIV

December 28

If we savor the good times in youth, we can enjoy them again in old age.

ONCE UPON A SUMMER PP. 14, 15

They shall abundantly utter the memory of thy great goodness.

PSALM 145:7 KJV

January 5

Just as we all have individual preferences, we also have individual gifts.

WHEN BREAKS THE DAWN PP. 20-25

For as in one body we have many members, and not all the members have the same function, so we, who are many, are one body in Christ, and individually we are members one of another.

ROMANS 12:4 NRSV

December 27

𝓤gly feelings that we try to hide inside us eventually surface as ugly behavior.

ONCE UPON A SUMMER PP. 15,16

The light shines in darkness, and the darkness did not overcome it.

JOHN 1:5 NRSV

January 6

Someday our Lord will return, and He wants us to work while we await Him.

WHEN COMES THE SPRING pp. 212,213

For the Lord is righteous, he loves righteous deeds; the upright shall behold his face.

PSALM 11:7 NRSV

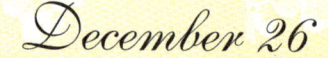

December 26

We can expect big trouble when we try to answer our own prayers.

Once Upon a Summer pp. 24,25

For your Father knows what you need before you ask him.

Matthew 6:8 kjv

January 7

𝒥esus makes Christmas special for us, so we make it special for others.

SPRING'S GENTLE PROMISE PP. 133,134

Glory to God in the highest, and on earth peace, good will toward men.

LUKE 2:14 KJV

December 25

The blessing of an earthly family gives us only a hazy picture of the blessing in God's heavenly family.

ONCE UPON A SUMMER P. 72

Children's children are the crown of old men; and the glory of children are their fathers.

PROVERBS 17:6 KJV

January 8

Giving ourselves, as God did, gives real meaning to Christmas.

Love's Unending Legacy p.83

For you know the grace of our Lord Jesus Christ, that though He was rich, yet for your sakes He became poor, that you through His poverty might become rich.

2 Corinthians 8:9 NKJV

December 24

Letting go of earthly attachments is the only way to hold onto God.

THE WINDS OF AUTUMN P. 117

Father, into thy hands I commend my spirit.

LUKE 23:46 KJV

January 9

Love that gives the greatest pleasure can cause the greatest pain.

LOVE'S ENDURING PROMISE P. 18

We know love by this, that he laid down his life for us—and we ought to lay down our lives for one another.

JOHN 3:16 NRSV

December 23

Whatever our job, God's will for us is to do our best.

WINTER IS NOT FOREVER P. 63

And whatsoever ye do in word or deed, do all in the name of the Lord Jesus, giving thanks to God and the Father by him.

COLOSSIANS 3:17 KJV

January 10

The mystery and miracle of the incarnation makes every day a Christmas celebration for the believer.

THE WINDS OF AUTUMN pp. 133,134

I bring you good tidings of great joy, which shall be to all people.

LUKE 2:10 KJV

December 22

When our load is light, it's time to carry someone else's.

ONCE UPON A SUMMER PP. 95, 96

As God's chosen ones,...clothe yourselves with compassion, humility, meekness, and patience.

COLOSSIANS 3:12 NRSV

January 11

Those who suffer the most often know the most about God's goodness.

When Calls the Heart pp. 128,129

But he knows the way that I take; when he has tested me, I will come forth as gold.

Job 23:10 niv

December 21

Grief is a natural and healthy emotion when a loved one dies, but self-pity helps no one.

LOVE COMES SOFTLY PP. 13,14

Though he cause grief, yet will he have compassion according to the multitude of his mercies.

LAMENTATIONS 3:32 KJV

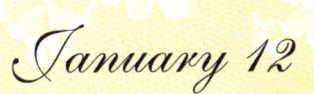

January 12

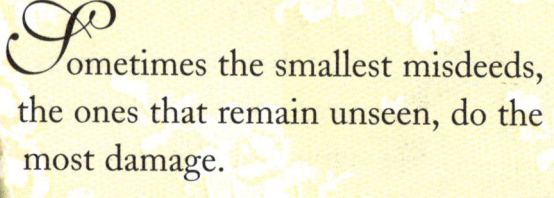

Sometimes the smallest misdeeds, the ones that remain unseen, do the most damage.

WHEN CALLS THE HEART PP. 141-147

My salvation and my honor depend on God.... Pour out your hearts to him, for God is our refuge.

PSALM 62:7,8 NRSV

December 20

We do not always know the reasons for what God does and doesn't do, but in the end we'll see that He was always right.

ONCE UPON A SUMMER PP. 117,118

At the name of Jesus every knee should bow.

PHILIPPIANS 2:10 KJV

January 13

Rules and laws are not always the best way to encourage good behavior.

WHEN CALLS THE HEART pp. 95,96

Create in me a clean heart, O God; and renew a right spirit within me.

PSALM 51:10 KJV

December 19

Discomfort may be the prelude
to a blessed event.

Spring's Gentle Promise pp. 159,160

*We know that in all things God works for
the good of those who love him.*

Romans 8:23 niv

January 14

Sometimes our worst fears are based on misinformation or misunderstanding.

When Calls the Heart pp. 79-83

But I will sing of your strength, in the morning I will sing of your love; for you are my fortress, my refuge in times of trouble.

Psalm 59:16 niv

December 18

Wrapping ourselves in bitterness is like using a blanket of poison ivy; it's warm at first but painful in the end.

Once Upon a Summer p. 122

I consider that our present sufferings are not worth comparing with the glory that will be revealed in us.

Romans 8:18 NIV

January 15

*H*ouses, weapons, and our own wits give us an illusion of safety and help us feel secure, but in the end, our only security is God.

When Calls the Heart pp. 77,78

But you, O Lord, are a shield around me, my glory, and the one who lifts up my head.

Psalm 3:4 nrsv

December 17

Each of us must choose what to remember—the good or the bad times of life.

ONCE UPON A SUMMER PP. 122-124

No eye has seen, nor ear has heard, nor the human heart conceived, what God has prepared for those who love him.

1 CORINTHIANS 2:9 NRSV

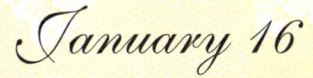

January 16

It is wise to make provision for physical safety, but it is even more important to make provision for the safety of the soul.

When Calls the Heart pp. 74-76

So we fix our eyes not on what is seen, but on what is unseen. For what is seen is temporary, but what is unseen is eternal.

2 Corinthians 4:18 NIV

December 16

How we respond to hurt determines whether our spirits will grow and bloom or wither and die.

Once Upon a Summer pp.124,125

Though he slay me, yet will I trust him.

Job 13:15 kjv

January 17

*People who try to "do us in"
may sometimes be doing us a favor.*

WHEN CALLS THE HEART PP. 60,61

*Even though you intended to do harm to me,
God intended it for good.*

GENESIS 50:20 NRSV

December 15

If we nurture love, it will destroy bitterness; if we nurture bitterness, it will destroy love.

Once Upon a Summer p. 125

But the fruit of the Spirit is love, joy, peace, patience, kindness, goodness, faithfulness, gentleness and self-control.

Galatians 5:22,23 niv

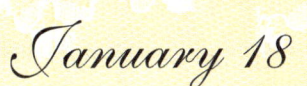

January 18

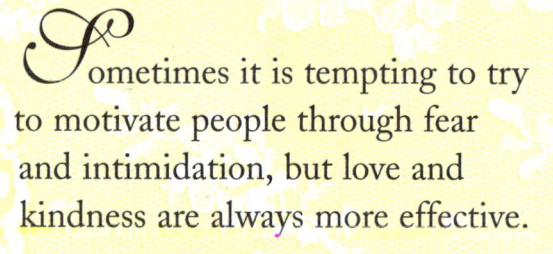

Sometimes it is tempting to try to motivate people through fear and intimidation, but love and kindness are always more effective.

WHEN CALLS THE HEART PP. 71, 72

As God's chosen ones, holy and beloved, clothe yourselves with compassion, kindness, humility, meekness, and patience.

COLOSSIANS 3:12 NRSV

December 14

*W*hat seems unimportant one day may be of utmost significance the next.

Once Upon a Summer pp. 146,147

He is not here, but is risen: remember how he spoke to you when he was still in Galilee.

Luke 24:6 nkjv

January 19

Showing kindness to others is one of the nicest things we can do for ourselves.

When Calls the Heart pp. 70,71

In response to all he has done for us, let us outdo each other in being helpful and kind to each other.

Hebrews 10:24 TLB

December 13

If we use our authority to walk on people, we can't expect them to stand on their own two feet.

WINTER IS NOT FOREVER PP. 68,69

Therefore encourage one another and build each other up.

1 THESSALONIANS 5:11 NIV

January 20

Being alone does not necessarily mean being lonely. In solitude we are more likely to hear God's sweetest songs.

WHEN CALLS THE HEART PP. 68,69

Surely I am with you always, to the very end of the age.

MATTHEW 28:20 NIV

December 12

When we follow God, people may question our direction.

ONCE UPON A SUMMER PP. 154, 155

Do not conform any longer to the pattern of this world, but be transformed by the renewing of your mind.

ROMANS 12:2 NIV

January 21

The peacefulness of God's creation reminds us of the spiritual peace we have when we live in obedience to Him.

WHEN CALLS THE HEART PP. 73,74

Great peace have those who love your law;
nothing can make them stumble.

PSALM 119:165 NRSV

December 11

The old story of God's grace should be new and fresh to us every day.

ONCE UPON A SUMMER PP. 159,160

But grow in the grace and knowledge of our Lord and Savior Jesus Christ. To him be glory both now and forever!

2 PETER 3:18 NIV

January 22

Fear may accompany new thoughts and ideas, but still we need to pursue them to determine whether or not they are for our good.

WHEN CALLS THE HEART pp. 16,17

Our steps are made firm by the Lord, when he delights in our way.

PSALM 37:23 NRSV

December 10

Confessing sin does more than just "patch up" our lives; it gives us a brand new start.

Once Upon a Summer pp. 163-165

If we confess our sins, He is faithful and just to forgive us our sins and to cleanse us from all unrighteousness.

1 John 1:9 nkjv

January 23

Children who learn spiritual truths early can be trusted to make wise decisions as they grow older.

WHEN CALLS THE HEART PP. 15,16

Train up a child in the way he should go: and when he is old, he will not depart from it.

PROVERBS 22:6 KJV

December 9

When our vision comes from God, there is no doubt that we can accomplish it.

Once Upon a Summer pp. 165,166

The one who calls you is faithful and he will do it.

1 Thessalonians 5:24 niv

January 24

A certain kind of restlessness is inevitable for believers because we can never quite feel at home on earth.

When Calls the Heart pp. 13,14

I go to prepare a place for you. And...I will come again and receive you to Myself.

John 14:2,3 nkjv

December 8

If we accept a rumor as fact, we encourage rumor spreaders, making it more likely that we too will become victims of untrue rumors.

Once Upon a Summer pp. 167,168

One who is trustworthy in spirit keeps a confidence.

Proverbs 11:13 nrsv

January 25

The happiest ending of all is when we are home with the ones we love and the One who loves us.

Love Finds a Home pp. 217,218

That you, being rooted and grounded in love, may be able to comprehend...the love of Christ which passes knowledge.

Ephesians 3:17-19 nkjv

December 7

*W*hen it comes to faith, it takes a combination of both working at it, and receiving it as a gift.

LOVE'S ABIDING JOY PP. 178,179

Through faith [they] subdued kingdoms, wrought righteousness, obtained promises, stopped the mouths of lions.

HEBREWS 11:33 KJV

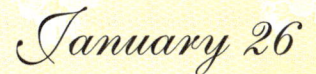

January 26

$\mathcal{G}$iving to others what is rightfully ours is a good indication that we are following Christ's example.

Love Finds a Home pp. 191,192

Give, and it will be given to you. A good measure, pressed down, shaken together and running over, will be poured into your lap.

Luke 6:38 niv

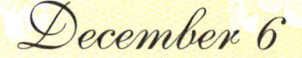

December 6

The loss that we dread sometimes brings us more than we had before.

ONCE UPON A SUMMER P. 196

I regard everything as loss because of the surpassing value of knowing Christ Jesus my Lord.

PHILIPPIANS 3:8 NRSV

January 27

God has a place of service for every person willing to serve.

LOVE FINDS A HOME PP. 181,182

Like good stewards of the manifold grace of God, serve one another with whatever gift each of you has received.

1 PETER 4:10 NRSV

December 5

When someone's good reputation needs defending, it is not the time for silence.

Once Upon a Summer pp. 176,177

To every thing there is a season,...A time to keep silence, and a time to speak.

Ecclesiastes 3:1,7 kjv

January 28

When we question a person's motives for doing good, we do that person and ourselves an injustice.

Love Comes Softly pp. 60,61

Truly God is good to the upright, to those who are pure in heart.

Psalm 73:1 nrsv

December 4

Patience keeps us from running ahead of God. Alertness keeps us from missing His opportunities.

Once Upon a Summer pp. 190-192

As we have therefore opportunity, let us do good unto all men.

Galatians 6:10 kjv

January 29

*W*hen an old friend is also a new friend, the pleasure doubles.

Love Finds a Home pp. 147,148

A friend loves at all times.

Proverbs 17:17 nkjv

December 3

When we get what we ask for we may lose what we love.

Once Upon a Summer p. 175

Delight thyself also in the Lord; and he shall give thee the desires of thine heart.

Psalm 37:4 kjv

January 30

We may think that having more possessions will ease our burdens, but it's more likely that the possessions themselves will become a burden.

Love Finds a Home pp. 111,112

Cast your burden on the Lord and He shall sustain you.

Psalm 55:22 nkjv

December 2

I will praise You, O Lord, with my whole heart; I will tell of all Your marvelous works. I will be glad and rejoice in You; I will sing praise to Your name, O Most High.

PSALM 9:1,2 NKJV

January 31

When we're uncertain about what to do, waiting may be the wisest response.

LOVE FINDS A HOME PP. 104,105

Wait on the Lord: be of good courage, and he shall strengthen thine heart: wait, I say, on the Lord.

PSALM 27:14 KJV

December 1

Accepting God's love enables us to love others.

Once Upon a Summer pp. 200, 201

We know love by this, that he laid down his life for us—and we ought to lay down our lives for one another.

1 John 3:16 nrsv

February 1

O Lord God Almighty, who is like you? You are mighty, O Lord, and your faithfulness surrounds you. Righteousness and justice are the foundation of your throne; love and faithfulness go before you.

Psalm 89:8,14 NIV

November 30

Love takes risks.

ONCE UPON A SUMMER PP. 199,200

[Love] beareth all things, believeth all things, hopeth all things, endureth all things.

1 CORINTHIANS 13:7 KJV

February 2

Unrealistic expectations may lead to unexpected disappointment.

Love's Unfolding Dream pp. 87,88

I know what it is to be in need, and I know what it is to have plenty. I have learned the secret of being content in any and every situation.

Philippians 4:12 niv

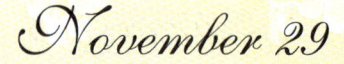

November 29

We all want peace, but few of us are willing to give up our pride and self-ambition to get it.

ONCE UPON A SUMMER P. 198

The mind of sinful man is death, but the mind controlled by the Spirit is life and peace.

ROMANS 8:6 NIV

February 3

The only way to tip God's scales in our favor is to get on the side with Jesus.

Love Finds a Home p. 93

I am the way and the truth and the life. No one comes to the Father except through me.

John 14:6 niv

November 28

What we consider "bad luck" may be part of God's sovereign plan.

THE WINDS OF AUTUMN PP. 60,61

The Lord makes poor and makes rich;
He brings low, and lifts up.

1 SAMUEL 2:7 NKJV

February 4

*W*hen we belong to God, the problem of finding our place in the world is only a temporary one.

LOVE FINDS A HOME PP. 84,85

Your goodness and unfailing kindness shall be with me all my life, and afterwards I will live with you forever in your home.

PSALM 23:6 TLB

November 27

What seems important in youth
may seem silly later.

THE WINDS OF AUTUMN PP. 63,64

In length of days [is] understanding.

JOB 12:12 KJV

February 5

In a short time, what is happening today will be the past you fondly remember.

Love Finds a Home pp. 68,69

I remember the days of long ago; I meditate on all your works and consider what your hands have done.

Psalm 143:5 niv

November 26

When a sincere compliment comes to mind, don't hesitate to give it.

THE WINDS OF AUTUMN PP. 64,65

Encourage one another daily, as long as it is called Today.

HEBREWS 3:13 NIV

February 6

Unimpressive people can make lasting impressions with a simple act of kindness.

LOVE FINDS A HOME PP. 18,19

But the fruit of the Spirit is love, joy, peace, longsuffering, gentleness, goodness, faith.

GALATIANS 5:22 KJV

November 25

*W*hat makes us miserable today
may have us laughing tomorrow.

THE WINDS OF AUTUMN P. 65

*Weeping may remain for a night, but
rejoicing comes in the morning.*

PSALM 30:5 NIV

February 7

Satan doesn't always pursue us like a hunter with a deadly weapon; sometimes he lures us like a trout fisherman with an irresistible fly.

Love Takes Wing p. 218

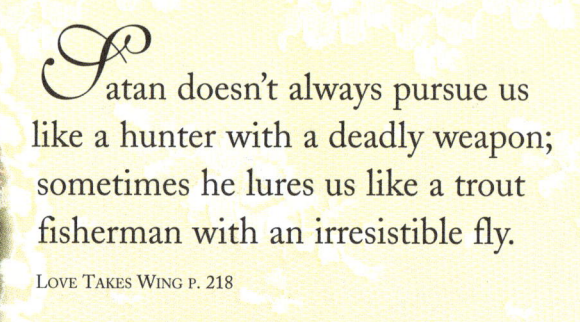

I have taught you the way of wisdom; I have led you in the paths of uprightness.

Proverbs 4:11 nrsv

November 24

$\mathcal{O}$ne person who refuses to listen to gossip can keep it from spreading.

THE WINDS OF AUTUMN P. 81

Whatever is true, whatever is noble, whatever is right, whatever is pure, whatever is lovely...think about such things.

PHILIPPIANS 4:8 NIV

February 8

When nothing seems satisfying,
we may be looking for satisfaction
in something other than God.

LOVE TAKES WING PP. 216,217

*As for me, I will behold thy face in
righteousness: I shall be satisfied, when
I awake, with thy likeness.*

PSALM 17:15 KJV

November 23

Ridicule and scorn do not help people improve.

THE WINDS OF AUTUMN PP. 87,88

Be peaceable and considerate,...show true humility toward all men.

TITUS 3:2 NIV

February 9

If we don't make poor people feel welcome, maybe our standards are different from God's.

LOVE'S UNFOLDING DREAM P. 165

The Lord is good to all; he has compassion on all he has made.

PSALM 145:9 NIV

November 22

$\mathcal{E}$very day we meet people whose eternal destiny may be affected by what we do or say.

THE WINDS OF AUTUMN pp. 99,100

Each of us should please his neighbor for his good, to build him up.

ROMANS 15:2 NIV

February 10

Beauty outside is no guarantee of warmth inside.

Love Takes Wing pp. 173, 174

Let your adornment be the inner self with the lasting beauty of a gentle and quiet spirit, which is very precious in God's sight.

1 Peter 3:4 nrsv

November 21

Mixing lies with truth is one of the oldest and most dangerous forms of deception.

The Winds of Autumn pp. 112,113

We stand in the presence of God as we speak and so we tell the truth.

2 Corinthians 4:2 tlb

February 11

When life seems to be going along just beautifully and trouble free, that's the time to watch out for temptation.

LOVE TAKES WING PP.151-157

God is faithful.... When you are tempted, he will also provide a way out so that you can stand up under it.

1 CORINTHIANS 10:13 NIV

November 20

Learn from the past, work for the present, and plan for the future.

WINTER IS NOT FOREVER pp. 90,91

Those who plan what is good find love and faithfulness.

PROVERBS 14:22 NIV

February 12

𝒜 heavy heart weighs more than any other burden.

Love Takes Wing pp. 145,146

Come to me, all you who are weary and burdened, and I will give you rest.

Matthew 11:28 niv

November 19

It is natural to defend ourselves.
It is spiritual to trust God to defend us.

The Winds of Autumn pp. 119,120

But love your enemies, do good to them....
Be merciful, just as your Father is merciful.

Luke 6:35,36 NIV

February 13

Human effort can bring people together physically, but only God's effort can bring them together spiritually.

Love Takes Wing pp. 137,138

If we walk in the light, as he is in the light, we have fellowship one with another.

1 John 1:7 kjv

November 18

Spiritual maturity, like physical maturity, brings added responsibility.

SPRING'S GENTLE PROMISE 13,14

When I became an adult, I put an end to childish ways.... Now I know only in part; then I will know fully.

1 CORINTHIANS 13:11,12 NRSV

February 14

*G*etting people inside the same house doesn't mean there is unity.

Love Takes Wing pp. 98,99

How wonderful it is, how pleasant, when brothers live in harmony!

Psalm 133:1 tlb

November 17

*O*nly Jesus can bring freshness and purity into our lives.

The Winds of Autumn pp. 127,128

Wash me, and I shall be whiter than snow.

Psalm 51:7 kjv

February 15

We cannot make people change, but we can make it as easy as possible for them to do so.

LOVE TAKES WING PP. 97,98

Gently and humbly help [others] back onto the right path.

GALATIANS 6:1 TLB

November 16

If we allow jealousy any space in our lives, it swells until we explode in rage.

THE WINDS OF AUTUMN PP. 128,129

Love is patient, love is kind. It does not envy.... It always protects, always trusts, always hopes, always perseveres.

1 CORINTHIANS 13:4,7 NIV

February 16

When there's division in God's family, the whole family suffers.

LOVE TAKES WING pp. 95,96

Make every effort to keep the unity of the Spirit through the bond of peace.

EPHESIANS 4:3 NIV

November 15

*God's boundless creativity
resulted in endless diversity.
Therefore, those who are different
are not necessarily wrong.*

WHEN CALLS THE HEART PP. 113,114

*We, who are many, are one body in Christ....
We have gifts that differ according to the
grace given to us.*

ROMANS 12:5,6 NRSV

February 17

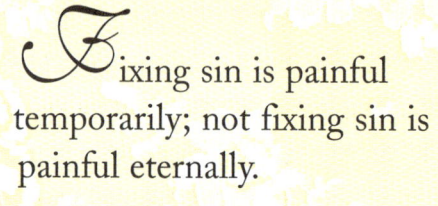

Fixing sin is painful temporarily; not fixing sin is painful eternally.

Love Takes Wing p. 85

No discipline seems pleasant at the time, but painful. Later on, however, it produces a harvest of righteousness and peace for those who have been trained by it.

Hebrews 12:11 niv

November 14

A solid foundation of spiritual truth helps us understand the natural world.

THE WINDS OF AUTUMN pp. 145,146

The creation itself will be liberated...and brought into the glorious freedom of the children of God.

ROMANS 8:21 NIV

February 18

Time seems to go faster the older we get because each additional year is a smaller percentage of the total time we have lived.

LOVE TAKES WING PP.42,43,73,74

I was young and now I am old, yet I have never seen the righteous forsaken.

PSALM 37:25 NIV

November 13

Each of us must choose whether to believe man and doubt God or to believe God and doubt man.

THE WINDS OF AUTUMN PP. 147,148

Let God be true, and every man a liar.

ROMANS 3:4 NIV

February 19

It is impossible to lose our bitterness without finding God first.

LOVE'S UNFOLDING DREAM pp. 209-214

I love them that love me; and those that seek me early shall find me.

PROVERBS 8:17 KJV

November 12

We need lean times to teach us to lean on God.

SPRING'S GENTLE PROMISE P. 176

And I will restore to you the years that the locust hath eaten.... And ye shall eat in plenty, and be satisfied, and praise the name of the Lord your God.

JOEL 2:25,26 KJV

February 20

Confidence in ourselves begins with confidence in God.

LOVE'S UNFOLDING DREAM pp. 218-221

This is the confidence that we have in him, that, if we ask any thing according to his will, he heareth us.

1 JOHN 5:14 KJV

November 11

Being open-minded is like driving a convertible; it's great under certain conditions, but if you don't know when to put the top on you'll be all wet.

THE WINDS OF AUTUMN PP. 152,153

And ye shall know the truth, and the truth shall make you free.

JOHN 8:32 KJV

February 21

When we're fighting an inner battle, we need strength from an outer source.

LOVE'S UNFOLDING DREAM pp. 206,207

Seek the Lord and his strength; seek his presence continually.

PSALM 105:4 NRSV

November 10

The words of God's created beings may fail under scrutiny, but the Word of the Creator never will.

THE WINDS OF AUTUMN PP. 152-154

Heaven and earth shall pass away, but my words shall not pass away.

MATTHEW 24:35 KJV

February 22

If we spend more time taking care of what we have and less time wanting what we don't have, we might find out that we already have what we want.

Love's Unfolding Dream pp. 197,198

Those who fear him have no want.... Those who seek the Lord lack no good thing.

Psalm 34:9,10 niv

November 9

It is better to be strangers than friends separated by sin.

THE WINDS OF AUTUMN PP. 161,162

Dear friend, do not imitate what is evil but what is good. Anyone who does what is good is from God.

3 JOHN 1:1 NIV

February 23

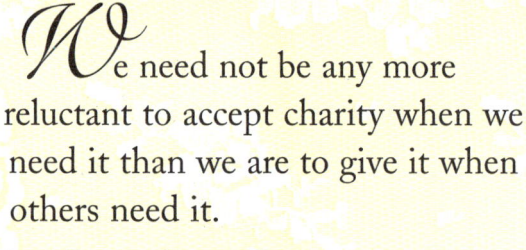

We need not be any more reluctant to accept charity when we need it than we are to give it when others need it.

LOVE'S UNFOLDING DREAM P. 197

Cast your bread upon the waters,
For you will find it after many days.

ECCLESIASTES 11:1 NKJV

November 8

*W*ishing evil for our enemies makes us equal to them.

THE WINDS OF AUTUMN P. 165

Try to show as much compassion as your Father does.

LUKE 6:36 TLB

February 24

When it comes to spiritual healing, adults often misunderstand the pain of God's treatment.

LOVE'S UNFOLDING DREAM pp. 183, 184

Rejoice that you participate in the sufferings of Christ, so that you may be overjoyed when his glory is revealed.

1 PETER 4:12 NIV

November 7

The majority of people never have the opportunity for a deathbed conversion.

THE WINDS OF AUTUMN pp. 170-173

Now is the day of salvation.

2 CORINTHIANS 6:2 KJV

February 25

We have nothing to give others except what God has given us.

LOVE TAKES WING pp. 206-208

A man can receive nothing, except it be given him from heaven.

JOHN 3:27 KJV

November 6

When the question is sorrow, time will answer it.

LOVE COMES SOFTLY PP. 176, 177

Ye shall be sorrowful, but your sorrow shall be turned into joy.

JOHN 16:20 KJV

February 26

When we feel as if we have nothing to do, perhaps God is giving us time to pray.

Love's Unfolding Dream pp. 158-161

The prayer of the righteous is powerful and effective.

James 5:16 nrsv

November 5

𝒫olite actions that cover hatred are evidence of hypocrisy, not Christianity.

THE WINDS OF AUTUMN PP. 180, 181

Our conscience testifies that we have conducted ourselves...in the holiness and sincerity that come from God.

2 CORINTHIANS 1:12 NIV

February 27

*W*ith some injuries, the body heals faster than the emotions.

LOVE'S UNFOLDING DREAM PP. 112,113

He heals the brokenhearted and binds up their wounds.

PSALM 147:3 NIV

November 4

I will rejoice in the Lord, I will be joyful in God my Savior. The Sovereign Lord is my strength; he makes my feet like the feet of a deer, he enables me to go on the heights.

Habakkuk 3:18,19 niv

February 28

When we see the least happening,
God may be doing the most work.

LOVE FINDS A HOME pp. 93,94

O the depth of the riches both of the wisdom and knowledge of God! how unsearchable are his judgments, and his ways past finding out!

ROMANS 11:33 KJV

November 3

You who dwell in the shelter of the Most High, who rest in the shadow of the Almighty, will say of the Lord, "My refuge and my fortress, my God, in whom I trust."

PSALM 91:15,16 NRSV

February 29

*W*hen our concern is genuine, the fear of being misunderstood shouldn't keep us from expressing it.

Love's Unfolding Dream pp. 43,44

Be ye all of one mind, having compassion one of another.

1 Peter 3:8 kjv

November 2

The first step toward knowing God's will is accepting it.

THE WIND OF AUTUMN pp. 183-185

And be not conformed to this world: but be ye transformed by the renewing of your mind.

ROMANS 12:2 KJV

March 1

When we pay close attention to our children's strengths and weaknesses, we are better able to "train them in the way they should go."

Love's Unfolding Dream pp. 58,59

Train up a child in the way he should go: and when he is old, he will not depart from it.

Proverbs 22:6 kjv

November 1

God has given us two ways to communicate—with words and with actions. We need both to do the job right.

Love's Enduring Promise pp. 12,13

Let us stop just saying we love people; let us really love them, and show it by our actions.

1 John 3:18 TLB

March 2

Every good and perfect gift is from above, coming down from the Father of heavenly lights, who does not change like shifting shadows.

JAMES 1:17 NIV

October 31

If our friends don't know God better for having known us, we are not a good friend.

THE WINDS OF AUTUMN pp. 191,192

Dear friend, I pray that you may enjoy good health and that all may go well with you, even as your soul is getting along well.

3 JOHN 2 NIV

March 3

God gives every believer a special gift and a special place to use it.

LOVE'S UNFOLDING DREAM PP. 22,23

We are God's workmanship, created in Christ Jesus to do good works, which God prepared in advance for us to do.

EPHESIANS 2:10 NIV

October 30

When it comes to understanding the origin of the earth, we must have faith in someone—God or man.

The Winds of Autumn pp. 192,193

Oh Lord,...I will exalt you...for in perfect faithfulness you have done marvelous things, things planned long ago.

Isaiah 25:1 niv

March 4

Doctors can postpone death, but only God can overcome it.

LOVE'S UNFOLDING DREAM PP. 13-20

I tell you the truth, whoever hears my word and believes him who sent me has eternal life...; he has crossed over from death to life.

JOHN 5:2 NIV

October 29

We cannot be forgiven if we refuse to forgive.

THE WINDS OF AUTUMN pp. 195-197

For if you forgive men when they sin against you, your heavenly Father will also forgive you.

MATTHEW 6:14 NIV

March 5

$\mathcal{W}$hat we invest in lives has lasting value.

LOVE'S UNENDING LEGACY PP. 221-224

Greater love has no one than this, that he lay down his life for his friends.

JOHN 15:13 NIV

October 28

In God's accounting ledger, our deeds of mercy have as much value as our cash.

The Winds of Autumn pp. 193,194

Blessed are the merciful: for they shall obtain mercy.

Matthew 5:7 kjv

March 6

$\mathcal{G}$rowing spiritually is like growing physically. Just when we think we've reached a new level of maturity, we revert to our old, immature behavior.

Love's Enduring Promise pp. 83,84

Therefore, if anyone is in Christ he is a new creation; old things have passed away; behold, all things have become new.

2 Corinthians 5:17 nkjv

October 27

Compassion for others comes when we see ourselves as God sees us.

THE WINDS OF AUTUMN pp. 197,198

The Lord...searches all hearts and examines deepest motives so he can give to each person his right reward.

JEREMIAH 17:10 TLB

March 7

Instead of crying over what has been taken from us, we should consider what has been given to us.

Love's Unending Legacy pp. 165,166

In everything give thanks: for this is the will of God in Christ Jesus concerning you.

1 Thessalonians 5:18 kjv

October 26

Death is frightening only because we know more about the physical world than the spiritual world.

THE WINDS OF AUTUMN pp. 200,201

Yea, though I walk through the valley of the shadow of death, I will fear no evil: for thou art with me.

PSALM 23:4 KJV

March 8

Buried under the biggest burden is a good place to find an even bigger blessing.

LOVE'S UNENDING LEGACY PP. 151,152

I will trust and not be afraid, for the Lord is my strength and my song; he is my salvation.

ISAIAH 12:12 TLB

October 25

To feel love gives pleasure to one; to express it gives pleasure to two.

THE WINDS OF AUTUMN pp. 201,202

Love each other...and take delight in honoring each other.

ROMANS 12:10 TLB

March 9

How can we say we trust God if we're afraid to obey Him?

Love's Unending Legacy p. 149

There is no fear in love, but perfect love casts out fear.

1 John 4:18 nrsv

October 24

$\mathcal{H}$arboring hate and bitterness is like spending a whole inheritance on vinegar.

THE WINDS OF AUTUMN PP. 202,203

Be humble and gentle. Be patient with each other, making allowance for each other's faults because of your love.

EPHESIANS 4:2 TLB

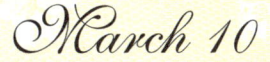

March 10

*W*e can be grateful that God's mercy is not determined by our merit.

Love's Unending Legacy pp. 145, 146

Not by works of righteousness which we have done, but according to his mercy he saved us.

Titus 3:5 kjv

October 23

We can change our behavior, but only God can change our motives.

THE WINDS OF AUTUMN P. 206

Search me, O God, and know my heart: try me and know my thoughts...and lead me in the way everlasting.

PSALM 139:23,24 KJV

March 11

When our idea of perfection comes from God, we don't pay much attention to appearance.

Love's Unending Legacy pp. 147, 178

Therefore you shall be perfect, just as your Father in heaven is perfect.

Matthew 5:48 nkjv

October 22

When we put God first, no one will feel as if he is in second place.

THE WINDS OF AUTUMN PP. 206,207

But seek ye first the kingdom of God, and his righteousness; and all these things shall be added unto you.

MATTHEW 6:33 KJV

March 12

We don't realize how bitterness weighs us down until we give it up.

Love's Unending Legacy p. 148

*You will keep him in perfect peace,
Whose mind is stayed on You,
Because he trusts in You.*

Isaiah 26:3 nkjv

October 21

How we leave the world is more important than how we enter it.

THE WINDS OF AUTUMN PP. 207, 208

He will give eternal life to those who patiently do the will of God.

ROMANS 2:7 TLB

March 13

*O*nly God, who sees from beginning to end, can determine what is fair.

Love's Unending Legacy p. 143

To the faithful you show yourself faithful, to the blameless your show yourself blameless, to the pure you show yourself pure.

Psalm 18:26 niv

October 20

*S*cientists have only the past on which to base their beliefs; with God, we have the future as well.

THE WINDS OF AUTUMN pp. 208,209

I am Alpha and Omega, the beginning and the end, the first and the last.

REVELATION 22:13 KJV

March 14

*S*ometimes it is easier to bear the pain ourselves than to watch someone we love suffer.

LOVE'S UNENDING LEGACY P. 139

Love suffers long and is kind.
1 CORINTHIANS 13:4 NKJV

October 19

Grief is inevitable and painful, but for the Christian it is accompanied by hope.

THE WINDS OF AUTUMN PP. 214,215

May the God of hope fill you with all joy and peace as you trust in him.

ROMANS 15:13 NIV

March 15

The only way to take control is to give it up.

Love's Unending Legacy p. 17

Whosoever will lose his life for my sake shall find it.

Matthew 16:25 kjv

October 18

When our lives are full of what we want, we have no room for what God wants to give us.

THE WINDS OF AUTUMN PP. 208-212

But lay up for yourselves treasures in heaven.... For where your treasure is, there your heart will be also.

MATTHEW 6:21 NKJV

March 16

𝒯he closer we are to something, the less we see of it. Only from God's perspective is everything seen.

LOVE'S UNENDING LEGACY PP. 123,124

For now we see in a mirror, dimly, but then face to face. Now I know in part, but then I shall know just as I also am known.

1 CORINTHIANS 13:12 NKJV

October 17

Confession is the only way to correct a corrupt conscience.

ONCE UPON A SUMMER PP. 36, 37

I said, "I will confess my transgressions to the Lord"—and you forgave the guilt of my sin.

PSALM 32:5 NIV

March 17

Building rapport is like learning first aid; it seems unnecessary until someone you love is dying.

Love's Unending Legacy pp. 130,131

Command them to do good...to be generous and willing to share. In this they will lay up treasure for themselves as a firm foundation for the coming age.

1 Timothy 6:18,19 NIV

October 16

When we pray with selfish motives we are asking God to do our will instead of surrendering to His.

THE WINDS OF AUTUMN pp. 209,210

Come near to God and he will come near to you...purify your hearts.... Humble yourselves before the Lord, and he will lift you up.

JAMES 4:8,10 NIV

March 18

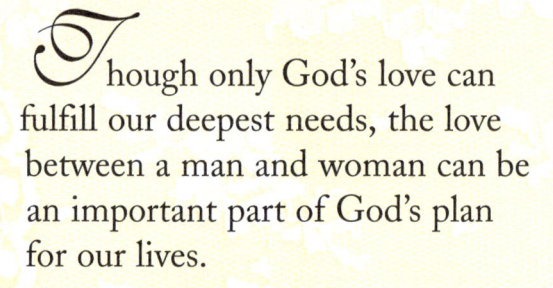

Though only God's love can fulfill our deepest needs, the love between a man and woman can be an important part of God's plan for our lives.

WHEN CALLS THE HEART pp. 216-221

Husbands, love your wives, just as Christ loved the church and gave himself up for her.
EPHESIANS 5:25 NIV

October 15

Surrendering to God gives us compassion for those who have not yet done so.

THE WINDS OF AUTUMN P. 216

Live in harmony with one another; do not be haughty.

ROMANS 12:16 NRSV

March 19

Having loved ones in heaven makes us more eager to get there.

Love's Unending Legacy p. 67

We who are still alive and are left will be caught up together with them in the clouds to meet the Lord in the air. And so we will be with the Lord forever.

1 Thessalonians 4:18 niv

October 14

Rest restores our strength; laziness diminishes it.

WINTER IS NOT FOREVER P. 92

In returning and rest you shall be saved; in quietness and in trust shall be your strength.

ISAIAH 30:15 NRSV

March 20

God meets our needs in unexpected ways.

LOVE'S UNENDING LEGACY pp. 43-45

And my God will meet all your needs according to his glorious riches in Christ Jesus.

PHILIPPIANS 4:19 NIV

October 13

*B*laming God for our disappointments is just another way of refusing to take responsibility for them.

THE WINDS OF AUTUMN PP. 215,216

Send forth your light and your truth, let them guide me.

PSALM 43:3 NIV

March 21

*Change makes life interesting;
changelessness makes it meaningful.*

LOVE'S UNENDING LEGACY PP. 28,29

*He changeth the times and the seasons....
I am the Lord, I change not.*

DANIEL 2:21; MALACHI 3:6 KJV

October 12

Physical freedom sometimes brings uncertainty; spiritual freedom always brings certainty.

WINTER IS NOT FOREVER P. 14

If the Son therefore shall make you free, ye shall be free indeed.

JOHN 8:36 KJV

March 22

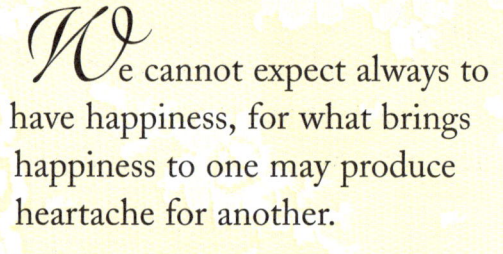

We cannot expect always to have happiness, for what brings happiness to one may produce heartache for another.

Love's Unending Legacy pp. 118,119

Be content with what you have, because God has said, "Never will I leave you; never will I forsake you."

Hebrews 13:5 niv

October 11

It is better to be uncertain for a while than to be wrong for a lifetime.

WINTER IS NOT FOREVER P. 27

Find rest, O my soul, in God alone.... Trust in him at all times, pour out your hearts to him, for God is our refuge.

PSALM 62:5,8 NIV

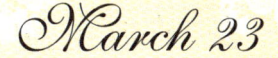

March 23

People should be able to see Christ in us, but we need to be careful that they not see us instead of Christ.

Love's Abiding Joy pp. 201,202

I am crucified with Christ: nevertheless I live; yet not I, but Christ liveth in me.

Galatians 2:20 kjv

October 10

A family is God's wall of
protection around children.

WINTER IS NOT FOREVER PP. 30-33

*Keep me as the apple of the eye, hide me
under the shadow of thy wings.*

PSALM 17:8 KJV

March 24

Curiosity may be a person's first step toward choosing a Christ-filled eternity.

Love's Abiding Joy pp. 199,200

I tell you the truth, whoever hears my word and believes him who sent me has eternal life...; he has crossed over from death to life.

John 5:24 niv

October 9

Fear often comes when we have the most to gain, because that's when we also have the most to lose.

Winter Is Not Forever pp. 30-33

The Lord is my light and my salvation—whom shall I fear? The Lord is the stronghold of my life—of whom shall I be afraid?

Psalm 27:1 niv

March 25

God may take extreme measures to put us where He wants us.

LOVE'S ABIDING JOY PP. 195,196

But the plans of the Lord stand firm forever, the purposes of his heart through all generations.

PSALM 33:11 NIV

October 8

People who care find ways to share other people's sorrow.

ONCE UPON A SUMMER PP. 120,121

Rejoice with those who rejoice, weep with those who weep.

ROMANS 12:15 NRSV

March 26

Everyone gets a last chance to accept God, but none of us knows when it will be.

LOVE'S ABIDING JOY P. 186

Now is the accepted time;...now is the day of salvation.

2 CORINTHIANS 6:2 KJV

October 7

When we're used to being first, it's not easy being last.

WINTER IS NOT FOREVER PP. 48,49

So the last will be first, and the first last: for many are called, but few chosen.

MATTHEW 20:16 NKJV

March 27

Chewing on pride doesn't make it easier to swallow.

LOVE'S ABIDING JOY PP. 152,153

*Though the Lord is on high,
Yet He regards the lowly;
But the proud He knows from afar.*

PSALM 138:6 NKJV

October 6

Having wrestled with a difficult decision, we will have more strength for the next one.

WINTER IS NOT FOREVER PP. 49, 50

I will go in the strength of the Lord God:
I will make mention of thy righteousness,
even of thine only.

PSALM 71:16 KJV

March 28

When we push people to make important decisions, we may unwittingly encourage them to make the wrong one.

LOVE'S ABIDING JOY PP. 177, 178

Listen to me; be silent, and I will teach you wisdom.

JOB 33:33 NIV

October 5

$\mathcal{G}$od has nothing to gain by misleading those who want to follow Him.

WINTER IS NOT FOREVER P. 63

Guide me in your truth and teach me, for you are God my Savior, and my hope is in you all day long.

PSALM 25:5 NIV

March 29

*W*hom we worship is more important than how we worship.

Love's Abiding Joy pp. 173,174

O Lord Almighty,...you alone are God over all the kingdoms of the earth. You have made heaven and earth.

Isaiah 37:16 niv

October 4

Let us know, let us press on to know the Lord; his appearing is as sure as the dawn; he will come to us like the showers, like the spring rains that water the earth.

Hosea 6:3 NRSV

March 30

A miraculously healed body lasts for a lifetime; a miraculously healed soul lasts for eternity.

Love's Abiding Joy pp. 154,155

The water that I shall give him shall be in him a well of water springing up into everlasting life.

John 4:14 KJV

October 3

I lift up my eyes to the hills—from where will my help come? My help comes from the Lord, who made heaven and earth.

Psalm 121:1,2 NRSV

March 31

Whenever anything bad happens we can start watching to see how God will use it for good.

Love's Abiding Joy pp. 157,158

All things work together for good to them that love God, to them who are the called according to his purpose.

Romans 8:28 kjv

October 2

The changes in nature remind us of the glorious transformation that's coming for all believers.

ONCE UPON A SUMMER PP. 93,94

We shall all be changed, in a moment, in the twinkling of an eye.

1 CORINTHIANS 15:51,52 KJV

April 1

God's answer to our prayers may be delayed by someone's stubbornness or pride.

Love's Abiding Joy pp. 171, 172

Devote yourselves to prayer, being watchful and thankful.

Colossians 4:2 NIV

October 1

Young lovers think love controls them; mature lovers know they can control love.

SPRING'S GENTLE PROMISE P. 130

Love...always protects, always trusts, always hopes, always perseveres. Love never fails.

1 CORINTHIANS 13:6-8 NIV

April 2

The Lord is my shepherd; I shall not want. He maketh me to lie down in green pastures: he leadeth me beside the still waters. He restoreth my soul: he leadeth me in the paths of righteousness for his name's sake.

PSALM 23:1-3 KJV

September 30

*W*hen anyone is forced to fight for his or her life, the human race loses more of God's image.

THE WINDS OF AUTUMN PP. 120,121

Love your enemies, do good to those who hate you,...pray for those who mistreat you.

LUKE 6:27,28 NIV

April 3

How precious it is, Lord, to realize that you are thinking about me constantly! I can't even count how many times a day your thoughts turn towards me.

PSALM 139:17 TLB

September 29

If we get God's approval daily, we don't have to fear His disapproval in the future.

Winter Is Not Forever p. 73

Do your best to present yourself to God as one approved...who correctly handles the word of truth.

2 Timothy 2:15 niv

April 4

Sowing seeds of doubt brings a harvest of confusion, misunderstanding, and hurt.

Once Upon a Summer pp. 167-169

Though the fig tree does not blossom, and no fruit is on the vines; though the produce of the olive fails and the fields yield no food,... yet I will rejoice in the Lord.

Habakkuk 3:17,18 nrsv

September 28

Things that cause us grief can be beautiful if we look at them from the right perspective—with our faces turned upward.

WINTER IS NOT FOREVER P. 79

May the favor of the Lord our God rest upon us; establish the work of our hands for us.

PSALM 90:17 NIV

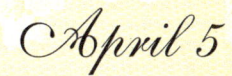

April 5

When a word of admonition is called for, we should make it kind, not critical.

Love's Abiding Joy p. 149

A word fitly spoken is like apples of gold in a setting of silver.

Proverbs 25:11 nrsv

September 27

𝓘f we try to possess another person, God is not in possession of us.

WINTER IS NOT FOREVER P. 70

Not lording it over those entrusted to you, but being examples.

1 PETER 5:3 NIV

April 6

The only safe way to walk into the future is with Someone who has already been there.

LOVE'S ABIDING JOY pp. 140,141

"I am the Alpha and the Omega," says the Lord God, who is and who was and who is to come, the Almighty.

REVELATION 1:8 NRSV

September 26

Giving ourselves is the most costly gift, and the most valuable.

Love's Abiding Joy p. 21

This is my body which is given for you.

Luke 22:19 kjv

April 7

How we respond to tragedy reveals how we have responded to God.

Love's Abiding Joy pp. 139,140

My grace is sufficient for you, for my power is made perfect in weakness.

2 Corinthians 12:9 NIV

September 25

If we selfishly consume all the good fruit God produces in our lives, we'll have only inferior seed to plant in the future.

Winter Is Not Forever pp. 92,93

Sow for yourselves righteousness, reap the fruit of unfailing love, and break up your unplowed ground: for it is time to seek the Lord.
Hosea 10:12 niv

April 8

When we talk with God regularly, we pick up a vocabulary that is foreign to people who don't know Him.

Love's Abiding Joy pp. 147, 148

We can see and understand only a little about God now...but someday we are going to see him in his completeness, face to face.

1 Corinthians 13:12 TLB

September 24

A bad influence is a good thing to avoid.

Winter Is Not Forever pp. 98,99

He who leads the upright along an evil path will fall into his own trap, but the blameless will receive a good inheritance.

Proverbs 28:10 niv

April 9

God never takes away anything we need to do His will.

LOVE'S ABIDING JOY PP. 138,139

And my God will meet all your needs according to his glorious riches in Christ Jesus.

PHILIPPIANS 4:19 NIV

September 23

It is difficult to keep a home together without love, and true love is impossible without God.

Winter Is Not Forever pp. 99,100

For I am convinced that nothing can ever separate us from his love.

Romans 8: 38 tlb

April 10

God can heal in at least two ways: making us better or taking us home.

LOVE'S ABIDING JOY PP. 128-130

So now...Christ shall be magnified in my body, whether it be by life, or by death.

PHILIPPIANS 1:20 KJV

September 22

If answered prayer surprises us,
our praying is more wishing
than believing.

WINTER IS NOT FOREVER PP. 105,106

And this is the confidence that we have in him, that, if we ask any thing according to his will, he heareth us.

1 JOHN 5:14 KJV

April 11

The small question "why?" requires an answer as big as God.

LOVE'S ABIDING JOY P. 118

God said to Moses, "I AM WHO I AM."

EXODUS 3:14 NIV

September 21

A good friend remembers what we were and sees what we can be.

WINTER IS NOT FOREVER PP. 113,114

Two are better than one.... If one falls down, his friend can help him up.

ECCLESIASTES 4:9,10 NIV

April 12

Reprimands don't always have to be harsh.

LOVE'S LONG JOURNEY P. 92

He tends his flock like a shepherd: He gathers the lambs in his arms and carries them close to his heart; he gently leads those that have young.

ISAIAH 40:11 NIV

September 20

People get their impressions of God from those who claim to follow Him.

Winter Is Not Forever p. 125

Be ye followers of me, even as I also am of Christ.

1 Corinthians 11:1 kjv

April 13

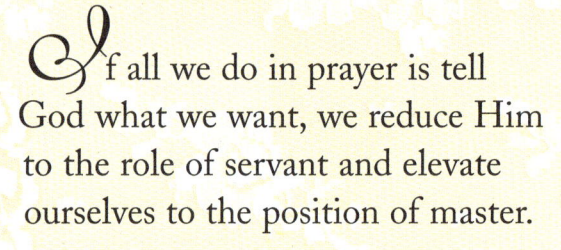

If all we do in prayer is tell God what we want, we reduce Him to the role of servant and elevate ourselves to the position of master.

Love's Abiding Joy p. 111

Yet, O Lord, you are our Father; we are the clay, and you are our potter; we are all the work of your hand.

Isaiah 64:8 kjv

September 19

The fear of death can lead to everlasting life.

WINTER IS NOT FOREVER PP. 125,126

For the wages of sin is death; but the gift of God is eternal life through Jesus Christ our Lord.

ROMANS 6:23 KJV

April 14

We should be more concerned about helping people find God than helping them find our church.

Love's Abiding Joy p. 87

And you will seek Me and find Me, when you search for Me with all your heart. I will be found by you, says the Lord.

Jeremiah 29:13 NKJV

September 18

*G*od doesn't mind us asking "why," but we don't always understand His answer right away.

LOVE'S ENDURING PROMISE PP. 32,33

Oh, the depth of the riches of the wisdom and knowledge of God! How unsearchable his judgments, and his paths beyond tracing out!

ROMANS 11:33 NIV

April 15

One of the best parts of growing old is enjoying all the pleasant memories we've taken time to store up.

Love's Abiding Joy p. 77

Even to your old age and gray hairs I am he, I am he who will sustain you. I have made you and I will carry you.

Isaiah 46:4 niv

September 17

*W*hen there's no way out of a situation, plow right through it.

Winter Is Not Forever pp. 133,134

I can do all things through Christ who strengthens me.

Philippians 4:13 nkjv

April 16

From the tunnel of suffering we have a choice of two exits—
bitterness and blessing.

Love's Abiding Joy pp. 75,76

Make the most of every opportunity you have for doing good. Don't act thoughtlessly, but try to find out and do whatever the Lord wants you to.

Ephesians 5:16,17 TLB

September 16

It is dangerous to get close to those who are far from God.

THE WINDS OF AUTUMN PP. 114-118

Blessed is the man that walketh not in the counsel of the ungodly.... But his delight is in the law of the Lord.

PSALM 1:1,2 KJV

April 17

God's will for the future is no different than it is for this moment.

WINTER IS NOT FOREVER PP. 13,14

Make the most of every opportunity you have for doing good. Don't act thoughtlessly, but try to find out and do whatever the Lord wants you to.

EPHESIANS 5:16,17 TLB

September 15

Good ideas may sound like crazy schemes when they threaten to disrupt our routines.

WINTER IS NOT FOREVER pp. 153-157

Then he said to them all, "If any want to become my followers, let them deny themselves and take up their cross daily and follow me."

LUKE 9:23 NRSV

April 18

*R*est restores our strength;
laziness diminishes it.

WINTER IS NOT FOREVER P. 92

Rest in the Lord, and wait patiently for him.

PSALM 37:7 KJV

September 14

God is big enough to handle small problems.

WINTER IS NOT FOREVER PP. 166,167

Let him have all your worries and cares, for he is always thinking about you and watching everything that concerns you.

1 PETER 5:7 TLB

April 19

When we fight our circumstances, rather than make peace with them, the circumstances inevitably win.

Love's Abiding Joy pp. 59,60

I believe that I shall see the goodness of the Lord in the land of the living. Wait for the Lord; be strong, and let your heart take courage.

Psalm 27:13,14 nrsv

September 13

Learning to get along with people is part of the preparation we need for heaven.

WINTER IS NOT FOREVER PP. 168,169

May the God who gives endurance and encouragement give you a spirit of unity among yourselves as you follow Christ Jesus.

ROMANS 15:5 NIV

April 20

Dwelling on "if onlys" only increases our dissatisfaction.

LOVE'S ABIDING JOY PP. 13,14

Fix your thoughts on what is true and good and right. Think about things that are pure and lovely.... Think about all you can praise God for and be glad about.

PHILIPPIANS 4:8 TLB

September 12

When voices join in song, lives blend in harmony.

WINTER IS NOT FOREVER PP. 181,182

Let the word of Christ dwell in you richly...as you sing psalms, hymns and spiritual songs with gratitude in your hearts to God.

COLOSSIANS 3:16 NIV

April 21

A fancy house may not be the best place to grow the best love.

LOVE'S LONG JOURNEY PP. 206, 207

The only thing that counts is faith expressing itself through love.

GALATIANS 5:6 NIV

September 11

Impatience can cause wise people to do foolish things.

WINTER IS NOT FOREVER PP. 182,183

As God's chosen ones, holy and beloved, clothe yourselves with compassion, kindness, humility, meekness, and patience.

COLOSSIANS 3:12 NRSV

April 22

Love can change the way we see things.

LOVE'S ABIDING JOY pp. 69,70

Love...bears all things, believes all things, hopes all things, endures all things. Love never fails.

1 CORINTHIANS 13:4,7,8 NKJV

September 10

The only good reason for making lots of money is to give it away.

WINTER IS NOT FOREVER pp. 192-194

As for those who in the present age are rich,... they are to do good, to be rich in good works, generous, and ready to share.

1 TIMOTHY 6:17,18 NRSV

April 23

We may be surprised at whom God sends to answer our prayers.

LOVE'S LONG JOURNEY PP. 196-200

Some have entertained angels unawares.

HEBREWS 13:2 KJV

September 9

*O*nly God can make sense out of senseless tragedies.

WINTER IS NOT FOREVER PP. 205,206

For as the heavens are higher than the earth, so are my ways higher than your ways, and my thoughts than your thoughts.

ISAIAH 55:9 KJV

April 24

A house can keep bad weather out, but only a home can keep people in.

LOVE'S LONG JOURNEY PP. 186,187

Lord, you have been our dwelling place throughout all generations.

PSALM 90:1 NIV

September 8

What belongs to God, we can never really lose.

WINTER IS NOT FOREVER PP. 207,208

Blessed be God, even the Father of our Lord Jesus Christ, the Father of mercies, and the God of all comfort; who comforteth us in all our tribulation.

2 CORINTHIANS 1:3,4 KJV

April 25

People we can pray with make the best friends.

LOVE'S LONG JOURNEY PP. 165,166

For where two or three are gathered in my name, I am there among them.

MATTHEW 18:20 NRSV

September 7

*W*hen God calls us to meet a need, He'll meet ours.

WINTER IS NOT FOREVER P. 209

I have chosen you, and ordained you, that ye should go and bring forth fruit, and that your fruit should remain.

JOHN 15:16 KJV

April 26

*O*nly God can keep all His promises.

LOVE'S LONG JOURNEY PP. 152,153

Not one word has failed of all his good promise.

1 KINGS 8:56 NRSV

September 6

The task of every believer is to fight the effects of sin in the world.

WINTER IS NOT FOREVER P. 216

Defend the cause of the weak and fatherless; maintain the rights of the poor and oppressed. Rescue the weak and needy; deliver them from the hand of the wicked.

PSALM 82:3,4 NIV

April 27

Accepting the truth is easier than living a lie.

LOVE'S LONG JOURNEY PP. 151,152

Guide me in your truth and teach me, for you are God my Savior, and my hope is in you all day long.

PSALM 25:5 NIV

September 5

A small task, done in obedience to God, is a big accomplishment.

WINTER IS NOT FOREVER pp. 217,218

But a poor widow came and put in two very small coins.... Jesus said, "...this poor widow has put more in the treasury than all the others."

MARK 12:42,43 NIV

April 28

Giving happiness brings happiness.

Love's Long Journey pp. 145-147

It is more blessed to give than to receive.

Acts 20:35 kjv

September 4

Learn from the past, work for the present, and plan for the future.

WINTER IS NOT FOREVER pp. 90,91

The Lord God is a sun and shield;
The Lord will give grace and glory;
No good thing will He withhold
From those who walk uprightly.

PSALM 84:11 NKJV

April 29

Adjusting to circumstances is the first step in overcoming them.

LOVE'S LONG JOURNEY PP. 130-132

I have learned to be content whatever the circumstances.

PHILIPPIANS 4:11 NIV

September 3

Show the wonder of your great love, you who save by your right hand those who take refuge in you.... Keep me as the apple of your eye; hide me in the shadow of Your wings.

Psalm 17:7,8 NIV

April 30

Jesus didn't find His disciples in church.

Love's Long Journey pp. 95,96

But God demonstrates his own love for us in this: While we were still sinners, Christ died for us.

Romans 5:8 niv

September 2

ℬeing in tune with God and His creation makes a song with beautiful harmony.

Spring's Gentle Promise p. 14

Sing to the Lord, all the earth;...for great is the Lord and most worthy of praise.

1 Chronicles 16:23,25 kjv

May 1

Blessings sometimes show up in unrecognizable disguises.

LOVE'S ABIDING JOY PP. 113,114

Praise be to the God and Father of our Lord Jesus Christ, who has blessed us in the heavenly realms with every spiritual blessing in Christ.

EPHESIANS 1:3 NIV

September 1

Praising God for health and prosperity keeps us from becoming proud.

SPRING'S GENTLE PROMISE P. 18

Bless the Lord, O my soul, and forget not all his benefits.

PSALM 103:2 KJV

May 2

Lay not up for yourselves treasures upon earth...but lay up for yourselves treasures in heaven.... For where your treasure is, there will your heart be also.

Matthew 6:19-21 KJV

August 31

When we only want what we need, we are on the right road to spiritual maturity.

Spring's Gentle Promise pp. 37,38

Delight yourself also in the Lord,
And He shall give you the desires
of your heart.

Psalm 37:4 NKJV

May 3

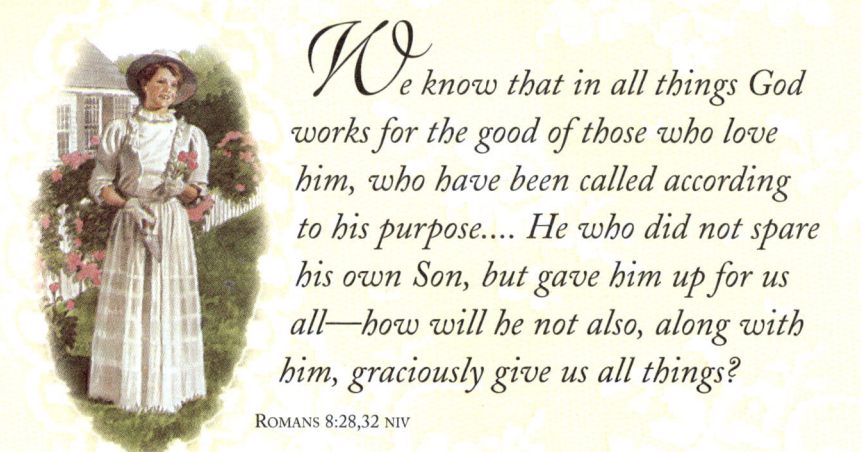

We know that in all things God works for the good of those who love him, who have been called according to his purpose.... He who did not spare his own Son, but gave him up for us all—how will he not also, along with him, graciously give us all things?

ROMANS 8:28,32 NIV

August 30

God gives more than we need so we can give to those in need.

SPRING'S GENTLE PROMISE P. 37

You glorify God by your obedience to the confession of the gospel of Christ and by the generosity of your sharing.

2 CORINTHIANS 9:13 NRSV

May 4

Experience teaches us when to wait and when to move forward.

Love's Long Journey pp. 62,63

You will show me the path of life; In Your presence is fullness of joy; At Your right hand are pleasures forevermore.

Psalm 16:11 nkjv

August 29

For thousands of years God has been working to undo the damage Abraham caused when he tried to help God.

Spring's Gentle Promise pp. 29,30

Then the angel of the Lord told [Hagar]... "You will have a son...his hand will be against everyone and everyone's hand against him...." So Hagar bore Abram a son.

Genesis 16:11,12,15 niv

May 5

Worrying about possible adversity is a waste of energy; but preparing for it is not.

Love's Long Journey pp. 57,58

Do not worry about anything, but in everything by prayer and supplication with thanksgiving let your requests be made known to God.

Philippians 4:6 NIV

August 28

Being the best we can be doesn't require having the best the world can make.

SPRING'S GENTLE PROMISE PP. 38,39

For the soul of every living thing is in the hand of God, and the breath of all mankind.

JOB 12:10 TLB

May 6

Growing up doesn't always mean leaving loved ones behind, but it does require leaving some loved things behind. As we take on responsibility, we must give up some of our freedom.

Love's Long Journey pp. 20,21

That we should no longer be children...but speaking the truth in love, may grow up in all things into Him.

Ephesians 4:14,15 nkjv

August 27

What we value reveals how valuable we are to God.

SPRING'S GENTLE PROMISE PP. 42,43

Let us fix our eyes on Jesus, the author and perfecter of our faith, who for the joy set before him endured the cross.

HEBREWS 12:2 NIV

May 7

A hard, crusty exterior may be hiding a tender, needy soul.

Love's Long Journey pp. 78,79

Cast your cares on the Lord and he will sustain you; he will never let the righteous fall.

Psalm 55:22 nrsv

August 26

Wanting what our peers want is jealousy; wanting what God wants is righteousness.

SPRING'S GENTLE PROMISE PP. 71,72

Since we live by the Spirit, let us keep in step with the Spirit.

GALATIANS 5:25 NIV

May 8

Busyness is an ally when it keeps away pain, but it is an enemy when it keeps us away from God.

Love's Long Journey p. 48

Keep your heart with all diligence, for out of it spring the issues of life.

Proverbs 4:23 NKJV

August 25

The right mate is worth the wait.

SPRING'S GENTLE PROMISE pp. 72,73

And Jacob loved Rachel, and said, I will serve thee seven years for Rachel thy younger daughter.

GENESIS 29:18 KJV

May 9

Waiting for the right time may be an excuse for doing the wrong thing.

LOVE'S LONG JOURNEY P. 49

Jesus said to him, "Let the dead bury their own dead, but you go and proclaim the kingdom of God."

LUKE 9:60 NIV

August 24

It's impossible to know the right person to marry without first knowing yourself.

SPRING'S GENTLE PROMISE P. 75

To get wisdom is to love oneself; to keep understanding is to prosper.

PROVERBS 19:8 NRSV

May 10

God takes away only as many of our fears as we give to Him.

LOVE'S LONG JOURNEY PP. 40,41

Whenever I am afraid, I will trust in you.

PSALM 56:3 NIV

August 23

When we wrap our arms around those who sorrow, we do so on behalf of Jesus, who would do it if He were here.

Spring's Gentle Promise, pp. 81,82

When others are troubled, needing our sympathy and encouragement, we can pass on to them this same help and comfort God has given us.

2 Corinthians 1:4 TLB

May 11

When we let God's Word seep into our lives little by little, crack by crack, it becomes a part of us.

Love's Long Journey pp. 21,22

I have hidden your word in my heart that I might not sin against you.

Psalm 119:11 niv

August 22

When we lose a person we love, having something he or she loved can help ease the pain of loss.

Spring's Gentle Promise pp. 86,87

And I will pray the Father, and he shall give you another Comforter, that he may abide with you for ever.

John 14:16 kjv

May 12

Trying to spare someone the worry of knowing the truth may cause them more worry about what's not true.

LOVE'S LONG JOURNEY PP. 53,54

I have not concealed...thy truth.

PSALM 40:10 KJV

August 21

If we fail to communicate, we also fail to understand.

SPRING'S GENTLE PROMISE PP. 114,115

Be kind and compassionate to one another.

EPHESIANS 4:32 NIV

May 13

A wise person can assess spiritual maturity and determine how much truth another can swallow.

Love's Enduring Promise pp. 170,171

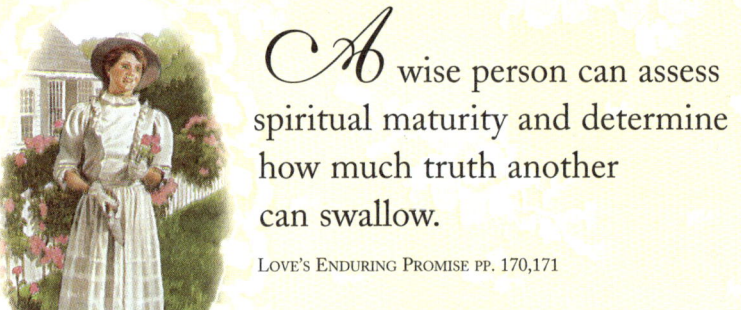

Like newborn babies, crave pure spiritual milk, so that by it you may grow up in your salvation.

1 Peter 2:2 niv

August 20

Being right but handling it wrong will make a bad situation worse. Being wrong and handling it right will make a bad situation better.

SPRING'S GENTLE PROMISE pp. 139,140

The Lord rewards every man for his righteousness and faithfulness.

1 SAMUEL 26:23 NIV

May 14

All the nurturing we do for children is for one purpose—so they'll no longer need us.

Love's Enduring Promise pp. 205, 206

As you know, we dealt with each one of you like a father with his children, urging and encouraging you and pleading that you lead a life worthy of God.

1 Thessalonians 2:11,12 NRSV

August 19

*F*riends may excuse our stupidity; only God can excuse our sin.

SPRING'S GENTLE PROMISE pp. 98,99

As far as the east is from the west, so far hath he removed our transgressions from us.

PSALM 103:12 KJV

May 15

No one ever gets so big, or so tough, that he has no need to cry.

LOVE'S ENDURING PROMISE PP. 196,197

I have heard thy prayer, I have seen thy tears.

2 KINGS 20:5 KJV

August 18

What seems accidental may be providential.

SPRING'S GENTLE PROMISE P. 107

You intended to harm me, but God intended it for good to accomplish what is now being done, the saving of many lives.

GENESIS 50:20 NIV

May 16

When everything we have belongs to God we don't have to fret about who's caring for it.

LOVE'S ENDURING PROMISE PP. 193,194

I know the one in whom I have put my trust, and I am sure that he is able to guard until that day what I have entrusted to him.

2 TIMOTHY 1:12 NRSV

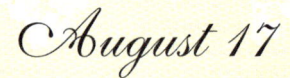

August 17

True love is more than sweet nothings.

SPRING'S GENTLE PROMISE PP. 115,116

Love is patient, love is kind. It does not envy, it does not boast, it is not proud.

1 CORINTHIANS 13:4 NIV

May 17

*O*ur ideas of perfection reveal our real values.

Love's Enduring Promise p. 175

Everyone who competes in the games goes into strict training. They do it to get a crown that will not last; but we do it to get a crown that will last forever.

1 Corinthians 9:25 NIV

August 16

𝒯hrough the eyes of marriage we see a picture of Christ and the church.

SPRING'S GENTLE PROMISE PP. 129,130

Husbands, love your wives, even as Christ also loved the church, and gave himself for it.

EPHESIANS 5:25 KJV

May 18

Judging ourselves by what others think of us is foolish, because others know little or nothing about us or our circumstances.

LOVE'S LONG JOURNEY PP. 19,20

There is therefore now no condemnation for those who are in Christ Jesus.

ROMANS 8:1 NRSV

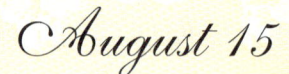

August 15

𝓑utting God out of our minds doesn't eliminate Him from our lives.

Once Upon a Summer pp. 147,148

Where can I go from your Spirit?
Where can I flee from you presence?
If I go up to the heavens, you are there;
if I make my bed in the depths you are there.

Psalm 139:7,8 niv

May 19

God can use our actions for good even when our reasons aren't all they should be.

LOVE'S ENDURING PROMISE PP. 167-169

The important thing is that in every way, whether from false motives or true, Christ is preached. And because of this I rejoice.

PHILIPPIANS 1:18 NIV

August 14

We never know what catastrophe may bring God's answer to our prayers.

SPRING'S GENTLE PROMISE PP. 98-100

Though I am surrounded by troubles...your power will save me. The Lord will work out his plans for my life.

PSALM 138:7,8 TLB

May 20

Wise words combined with good deeds is the most effective way to tell others why we love God.

LOVE'S ENDURING PROMISE P. 166

And whatever you do or say, let it be as a representative of the Lord Jesus.

COLOSSIANS 3:17 TLB

August 13

God sees more potential in us than we see in ourselves.

Spring's Gentle Promise p. 136

Ye have not chosen me, but I have chosen you.

John 15:16 kjv

May 21

When the unexpected catches us off guard, the Guard of the universe will catch us.

LOVE'S ENDURING PROMISE PP. 161,162

The eternal God is your refuge, and underneath are the everlasting arms.

DEUTERONOMY 33:27 NIV

August 12

We'll do better at keeping our earthly accounts balanced if we keep in mind that one day we will have to account to God.

WHEN COMES THE SPRING PP. 131,132

Every one of us shall give account of himself to God.

ROMANS 14:12 KJV

May 22

The way we choose to go around an obstacle will determine whether we move toward God or away from Him.

Love's Enduring Promise p. 146

If we live in the Spirit, let us also walk in the Spirit.

Galatians 5:25 nkjv

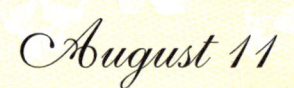

August 11

It is better to lose our pride than our temper.

Spring's Gentle Promise pp. 140,141

But the fruit of the Spirit is love, joy, peace, patience, kindness, goodness, faithfulness, gentleness and self-control.

Galatians 5:22,23 niv

May 23

Truth and tears can clear the way to a deep and lasting friendship.

LOVE'S ENDURING PROMISE pp. 137,138

A true friend is always loyal.

PROVERBS 17:17 TLB

August 10

Oneness in marriage makes us twice as strong and half as vulnerable.

SPRING'S GENTLE PROMISE pp. 154,155

The two shall become one — no longer two, but one!

MATTHEW 19:6 TLB

May 24

An education doesn't help us serve God's cause if it isolates us from those who need Him.

Love's Enduring Promise pp. 134,135

For we are what he has made us, created in Christ Jesus for good works, which God prepared beforehand to be our way of life.

Ephesians 2:10 nrsv

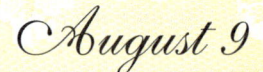

August 9

*W*hen we're irritable with others it may be because we're angry with ourselves.

Winter Is Not Forever p. 17

Above all, love each other deeply, because love covers over a multitude of sins.

1 Peter 4:8 niv

May 25

To communicate the Good News, we need to know more than the right words; we need to know the listener.

Love's Enduring Promise pp. 130,131

I count all things but loss for the excellency of the knowledge of Christ Jesus.

Philippians 3:8 kjv

August 8

If we don't know the sorrow of saying goodbye, we can never know the joy of saying hello.

SPRING'S GENTLE PROMISE PP. 163,164

Recalling your tears, I long to see you, so that I may be filled with joy.

2 TIMOTHY 1:4 NIV

May 26

We should try to find the good in people before we read it in their obituaries.

LOVE'S ENDURING PROMISE p. 124

Whatsoever things...are of a good report... think on these things.

PHILIPPIANS 4:8 KJV

August 7

Spiritual birth is sometimes a slow and painful process, but the joy of conversion makes it worthwhile.

Spring's Gentle Promise p. 170

Although you have not seen him, you love him; and even though you do not see him now, you believe in him and rejoice with an indescribable and glorious joy,

1 Peter 1:8 NRSV

May 27

*H*ow we pray reveals what we believe.

LOVE'S ENDURING PROMISE PP. 106,110

If we ask any thing according to his will, he heareth us.

1 JOHN 5:14 KJV

August 6

People who depend on nature for their livelihood know how dependent they are on God.

SPRING'S GENTLE PROMISE pp. 179,180

Sing unto the Lord with thanksgiving... who prepareth rain for the earth, who maketh grass to grow upon the mountains.

PSALM 147:7,8 KJV

May 28

lenty of people are examples of how not to live; few illustrate how we should live.

LOVE'S ENDURING PROMISE P. 100

Be a pattern...in your love, your faith, and your clean thoughts.

1 TIMOTHY 4:12 TLB

August 5

It is impossible to prove anything to someone who has chosen not to believe.

THE WINDS OF AUTUMN pp. 148,149

It is God who works in you to will and to act according to his good purpose.

PHILIPPIANS 2:13 NIV

May 29

What a few words can't say, a lifetime of action can.

Love's Unending Legacy pp. 198, 199

Little children, let us love, not in word or speech, but in truth and action.

1 John 3:18 nrsv

August 4

Now thanks be to God who always leads us in triumph in Christ, and through us diffuses the fragrance of His knowledge in every place. For we are to God the fragrance of Christ.

2 Corinthians 2:14,15 NKJV

May 30

Disappointment, in adults as well as in children, can lead to bad behavior.

Love's Enduring Promise pp. 82,83

In repentance and rest is your salvation, in quietness and trust is your strength.... The Lord longs to be gracious to you; he rises to show you compassion. For the Lord is a God of justice. Blessed are all who wait for him.

Isaiah 30:15,18 NIV

August 3

But this I call to mind, and therefore I have hope: The steadfast love of the Lord never ceases, his mercies never come to an end; they are new every morning; great is your faithfulness.

Lamentations 3:21-23 NRSV

May 31

We never know who's listening to what we say...or who's copying it.

Love's Enduring Promise p. 66

Be ye followers of me, even as I also am of Christ.

1 Corinthians 11:1 kjv

August 2

It is just as impossible to survive without water from heaven as it is to survive without water from earth.

SPRING'S GENTLE PROMISE P. 183

And the Lord shall guide thee continually, and satisfy thy soul in drought.

ISAIAH 58:11 KJV

June 1

Good fortune may bring quick reward, but only hard work brings reliable income.

LOVE'S ENDURING PROMISE P. 60

Work with your own hands,...that ye may have lack of nothing.

1 THESSALONIANS 4:11,12 KJV

August 1

Trying to carry too much may make us too weak to carry anything.

Spring's Gentle Promise p. 186

Take my yoke upon you and learn from me, for I am gentle and humble in heart, and you will find rest for your souls. For my yoke is easy and my burden is light.

Matthew 11:29,30 niv

June 2

Your heavenly Father knows your needs. He will always give you all you need from day to day if you will make the Kingdom of God your primary concern. So don't be afraid, little flock. For it gives your Father great happiness to give you the Kingdom.

Luke 12:30-32 TLB

July 31

A taste of what we don't have makes us discontent with what we do have.

SPRING'S GENTLE PROMISE PP. 184,185

I have learned the secret of being content in any and every situation, whether well fed or hungry, whether living in plenty or in want.

PHILIPPIANS 4:12 NIV

June 3

For God so loved the world, that he gave his only begotten Son, that whosoever believeth in him should not perish, but have everlasting life.

John 3:16 KJV

July 30

What we own is not as important as who owns us.

SPRING'S GENTLE PROMISE pp. 195,196

For you were bought at a price; therefore glorify God in your body and in your spirit, which are God's.

1 CORINTHIANS 6:20 NKJV

June 4

Doing right is one decision we can make without considering the consequences.

LOVE'S ENDURING PROMISE pp. 58,59

And when we obey him, every path he guides us on is fragrant with his loving-kindness and his truth.

PSALM 25:10 TLB

July 29

When our strength wanes, God's remains.

SPRING'S GENTLE PROMISE pp. 202,203

My grace is sufficient for thee: for my strength is made perfect in weakness.

2 CORINTHIANS 12:9 KJV

June 5

Stubbornness and selfishness go hand in hand. People who have one almost always have the other.

Love's Enduring Promise p. 50

Do nothing out of selfish ambition or vain conceit, but in humility consider others better than yourselves.

Philippians 2:3 niv

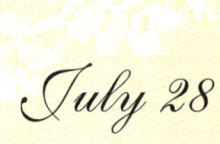

July 28

*W*hen the end is near,
so is God.

SPRING'S GENTLE PROMISE p. 203

I will not be afraid, for you are close beside me, guarding, guiding all the way.

PSALM 23:4 TLB

June 6

Whether or not God will answer our prayers is not a matter of question, but how He will answer may leave us wondering.

Love's Enduring Promise p. 54

The eyes of the Lord are on the righteous. And His ears are open to their prayers.

1 Peter 3:12 NKJV

July 27

We give ourselves because He gave himself.

SPRING'S GENTLE PROMISE PP. 212,213

And walk in love, as Christ also hath loved us, and hath given himself for us an offering and a sacrifice to God.

EPHESIANS 5:2 KJV

June 7

The ability to share a person's grief is a gift from God.

LOVE'S ENDURING PROMISE PP. 45,46

Therefore, as God's chosen people, holy and dearly loved, clothe yourselves with compassion, kindness, humility, gentleness and patience.

COLOSSIANS 3:12 NIV

July 26

God expressed His love for us in a personal letter that we are to share with the rest of the world.

SPRING'S GENTLE PROMISE PP. 211, 212

Let your light so shine before men, that they may see your good works, and glorify your Father which is in heaven.

MATTHEW 5:16 KJV

June 8

*W*hat causes one person great joy may cause another great sorrow.

WINTER IS NOT FOREVER pp. 126-128

Rejoice with those who rejoice, and weep with those who weep.

ROMANS 12:15 NKJV

July 25

When we don't see God working, we're looking in the wrong place.

SPRING'S GENTLE PROMISE p. 205

Now glory be to God who by his mighty power at work within us is able to do far more than we would ever dare to ask or even dream of.

EPHESIANS 3:20 TLB

June 9

God doesn't pry us away from our sins. He insists that we let go of them ourselves before He carries them away.

Love's Enduring Promise pp. 33,34

If we confess our sins, he is faithful and just to forgive us our sins, and to cleanse us from all unrighteousness.

1 John 1:9 kjv

July 24

*H*onesty and vulnerability
lead to camaraderie.

SPRING'S GENTLE PROMISE P. 213

*Don't just pretend that you love others:
really love them....and take delight in
honoring each other.*

ROMANS 12:9,10 TLB

June 10

Maturity teaches us the necessity of patience, but it's still difficult to achieve.

Love's Enduring Promise p. 39

When your patience is finally in full bloom, then you will be ready for anything, strong in character, full and complete.

James 1:4 TLB

July 23

Nothing happens to us that God hasn't already handled before.

SPRING'S GENTLE PROMISE PP. 218, 219

And God is able to make all grace abound to you, so that in all things at all times, having all that you need, you will abound in every good work.

2 CORINTHIANS 9:8 NIV

June 11

Having nice things doesn't make a person nice.

LOVE'S ENDURING PROMISE PP. 28,29

Let your adornment be the inner self with the lasting beauty of a gentle and quiet spirit, which is very precious in God's sight.

1 PETER 3:4 NRSV

July 22

Giving up what we think is ours allows God to give us what is His.

SPRING'S GENTLE PROMISE PP. 217-219

Whosoever shall lose his life for my sake,...
the same shall save it.

MARK 8:35 KJV

June 12

When we pray for what we want we should keep in mind that only God knows what we need.

LOVE'S ENDURING PROMISE PP. 24,25

If ye then...know how to give good gifts unto your children, how much more shall your Father which is in heaven give good things to them that ask him?

MATTHEW 7:11 KJV

July 21

*W*hen God gives us another chance, there's no risk involved.

SPRING'S GENTLE PROMISE pp. 220-222

From the fullness of his grace we have all received one blessing after another.

JOHN 1:16 NIV

June 13

Weariness caused by well-doing makes us feel worthwhile.

LOVE'S ENDURING PROMISE p. 20

Let us not become weary in doing good, for at the proper time we will reap a harvest if we do not give up.

GALATIANS 6:9 NIV

July 20

We never know which of the things we do will stay forever in our minds, so it's best to choose each action carefully.

Once Upon a Summer pp. 96,97

Let us draw near to God with a sincere heart in full assurance of faith, having our hearts sprinkled to cleanse us from a guilty conscience.

Hebrews 10:22 niv

June 14

Despite our stubbornness, God does not dismiss us from His thoughts.

When Calls the Heart p. 206

O Lord, you...know everything about me.... You both precede and follow me, and place you hand of blessing on my head. I can never be lost to your Spirit!

Psalm 139:1,5,7 TLB

July 19

Though it goes against our senses to think so, what seems to be a bad alternative may be the best one.

Love Comes Softly pp. 15,16

But God hath chosen the foolish things of the world to confound the wise; and God hath chosen the weak things of the world to confound the things which are mighty.

1 Corinthians 1:27 kjv

June 15

Getting things accomplished isn't nearly as important as taking time for love.

Love's Enduring Promise p. 17

The only thing that counts is faith expressing itself through love.

Galatians 5:6 niv

July 18

We can be grateful that God does indeed know us all by name; we too need all the help we can get.

LOVE COMES SOFTLY pp. 32,33

I have called you by your name. You are mine.
When you pass through the waters,
I will be with you.

ISAIAH 43:1,2 NKJV

June 16

With a sovereign God, things won't always go our way.

THE WINDS OF AUTUMN pp. 185,186

Abba, Father, all things are possible for You. Take this cup away from me; nevertheless, not what I will, but what You will.

MARK 14:36 NKJV

July 17

The most sensitive response may be silence.

Love Comes Softly pp. 18-20

Be still, and know that I am God.

Psalm 46:10 kjv

June 17

A quiet morning with a loving God puts the events of the upcoming day into proper perspective.

LOVE'S ENDURING PROMISE p. 12

Satisfy us in the morning with your unfailing love, that we may sing for joy and be glad all our days.

PSALM 90:14 NIV

July 16

Being religious doesn't always save us "a heap of trouble," but it ought to keep us from causing trouble for others.

Love Comes Softly pp. 23,24

In this world you will have trouble. But take heart! I have overcome the world.

James 1:27 kjv

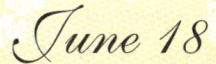

June 18

Mature love senses a loved one's need and reaches out immediately to meet it.

LOVE'S ENDURING PROMISE PP. 9,10

That their hearts might be comforted, being knit together in love, and unto all riches of the full assurance of understanding.

COLOSSIANS 2:2 KJV

July 15

$\mathcal{L}$ove comes when we take the time to understand and care for another person.

LOVE COMES SOFTLY PP. 25-31

If anyone gives even a cup of cold water to one of these little ones..., I tell you the truth, he will certainly not lose his reward.

MATTHEW 10:42 NIV

June 19

Seeing how God works in nature can help us understand how He works in our lives.

LOVE COMES SOFTLY PP. 179,180

Ever since the creation of the world his eternal power and divine nature, invisible though they are, have been understood and seen through the things he has made.

ROMANS 1:20 NRSV

July 14

Giving in to what may be unpleasant is better than giving up hope.

Love Comes Softly p. 17

For thou art my hope, O Lord God: thou art my trust from my youth.

Psalm 71:5 kjv

June 20

Strength comes in quietness.

LOVE COMES SOFTLY P. 179

In quietness and in confidence shall be your strength.

ISAIAH 30:15 KJV

July 13

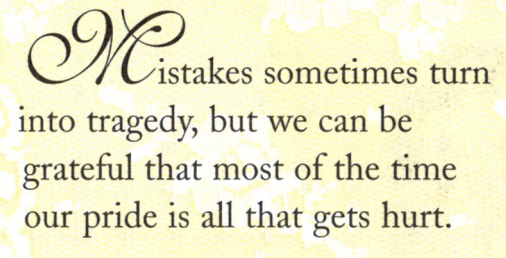

Mistakes sometimes turn into tragedy, but we can be grateful that most of the time our pride is all that gets hurt.

Love Comes Softly pp. 38,39

Though I am surrounded by troubles you will see me safely through.... The Lord will work out his plans for my life.

Psalm 138:7,8 tlb

June 21

$\mathcal{O}$ur motive for service must be to give, not to get.

THE WINDS OF AUTUMN PP. 174,175

By love serve one another.

GALATIANS 5:13 KJV

July 12

Sometimes we wish and pray for what we think will make us happy, not realizing that we already have it.

LOVE COMES SOFTLY P. 41

The eyes of your understanding being enlightened; that ye may know...the riches of the glory of his inheritance.

EPHESIANS 1:18 KJV

June 22

People, like children and seeds, have unique characteristics that require special handling and treatment.

Love Comes Softly p. 172

Even the very hairs of your head are all numbered. So don't be afraid; you are worth more than many sparrows.

Matthew 10:30,31 niv

July 11

*N*othing is so bad that we can't say a kind word about it.

Love Comes Softly pp. 47,48

Everything God created is good and...
[is to] be received with thanksgiving.

1 Timothy 4:4 kjv

June 23

Sharing God with others, unlike sharing anything else, does not diminish our portion.

Love Comes Softly pp. 166,167

Now you are the body of Christ, and each one of you is a part of it.

1 Corinthians 12:27 niv

July 10

A caring heart and a simple deed can relieve another's grief.

Love Comes Softly p. 54

He careth for you.

1 Peter 5:7 kjv

June 24

In his graciousness, God gives us many luxuries; we make a mistake when we consider them necessities.

Love Comes Softly pp. 153-155

So why do you worry about clothes? See how the lilies of the field grow.... Yet I tell you that not even Solomon in all his splendor was dressed like one of these.

Matthew 6:28,29 niv

July 9

𝒮ometimes our own sorrow so consumes us that we forget the needs of others.

Love Comes Softly pp. 58,59

Each of you should look not only to your own interests, but also to the interests of others.

Philippians 2:4 niv

June 25

When others don't know how to pray for themselves, God answers our prayers on their behalf.

Love Comes Softly pp. 149,150

Pray for each other.

James 5:16 kjv

July 8

*W*hen our days are filled with crying, we can trust that God, in time, will again bring laughter.

Love Comes Softly p. 59

Weeping may endure for a night, but joy cometh in the morning.

Psalm 30:5 kjv

June 26

It's natural to want to blame something or someone for bad circumstances, but doing so only gives us a handle with which to hang on to bitterness.

Love Comes Softly p. 140

Pursue peace with everyone, and the holiness without which no one will see the Lord.

Hebrews 12:14 nrsv

July 7

We think wealth will make life simpler, but it usually makes it more complicated.

Love Finds a Home pp. 168,169

He that trusteth in his riches shall fall: but the righteous shall flourish as a branch.

Proverbs 11:28 kjv

June 27

*L*ittle feelings are important, because they grow to be big attitudes.

Love Comes Softly pp. 148,149

Only the Lord knows! He searches all hearts and examines deepest motives so he can give to each person his right reward, according to his deeds—how he has lived.

Jeremiah 17:10 tlb

July 6

$\mathcal{L}$eading people to God by the way we live, rather than pushing them to acknowledge Him, can relieve their fear of approaching Him for the first time.

Love Comes Softly p. 82

Set an example for the believers in speech, in life, in love, in faith and in purity.

1 Timothy 4:12 niv

June 28

God's love doesn't always come waving flags. It too can "steal up on you gradually."

Love Comes Softly pp. 136,137

But God demonstrates His own love toward us, in that while we were still sinners, Christ died for us.

Romans 5:8 nkjv

July 5

Planning for the future is always better than lamenting the past.

LOVE COMES SOFTLY PP. 107,108

For I know the plans I have for you,...
plans to prosper you and not to harm you,
plans to give you hope and a future.

JEREMIAH 29:11 NIV

June 29

Intense pain often precedes immense pleasure.

LOVE COMES SOFTLY pp. 131-133

I take pleasure in infirmities:...when I am weak, then am I strong.

2 CORINTHIANS 12:10 KJV

July 4

Whom have I in heaven but you? And there is nothing on earth that I desire other than you. My flesh and my heart may fail, but God is the strength of my heart and my portion forever.

Psalm 73:25,26 NRSV

June 30

Having someone who understands is a great blessing for ourselves. Being someone who understands is a great blessing to others.

Love Comes Softly p. 116

Finally, all of you, have unity of spirit, sympathy, love for one another, a tender heart, and a humble mind.

1 Peter 3:8 nrsv

July 3